Table for One

21 Day Personal Journal

By Coco Roberts

Table for One

21 Day

Personal Journal

This idea came to me in my sleep, I woke up and wrote the idea in my phone. Each part of this was a vision, from the number of days, the name of the journal, and the photo. Will you spend twenty-one days with me?

Coco Roberts

Photographed by: A1 Monny

DJD Publications
Jacksonville, Florida
cococamwrites@aol.com

All rights reserved: This book is protected under the copyright laws of the United States of America. No part of this book may be reproduced or transmitted in any form or by any means – electronic or mechanical, including photocopying, recording or by any information storage and retrieved system without written permission from the authors, except for the inclusion of brief quotations in a review.

This is a work of fiction. Names, characters, places, businesses and incidents either are products of the author's imagination or are used fictitiously and are not to be construed as real. Any resemblance to a real person, living or dead, business establishments, actual events, locales, or organizations are entirely coincidental and not intended by the author.

DJD Publications Books are available at special discounts for bulk purchases. Contact: Coco at www.cocorobertsbooks.com

Copyright © 2021 Coco
ISBN #: 978-0-9861251-7-1
Library of Congress Control Number: 2021903746
Printed in the United States of America

Welcome to a Table for One; yes, this table is set just for you. It is said that it takes twenty-one days for something to become a habit and ninety days for it to become permanent. Well, in this journal, A Table for One, I would like for you to take the time to form a new habit of knowing yourself. I want you to be selfish for the next twenty-one days. and not allow anyone to sit at your table. You are more than welcome to share with them once you are done. As you prepare your table, I want you to go into this with an open mind and be willing to embrace change. Are you ready? Prepare your table, let's go!

But mine is just one seat
At the table.
-Jim Haslam

Day One

Day one is easy, take a minute or more if you would like. Place your feet on the floor, place your hands on your lap, and inhale the positive, exhale the negative. As you are breathing in (positive) think of something that you would like to be positive about. As you exhale (negative), think of something that you would like to let go of.

What did you inhale?

_____
_____
_____
_____
_____
_____
_____
_____
_____
_____
_____
_____
_____
_____
_____

What did you exhale?

Day Two

I am big on affirmations! If you've never affirmed yourself each day, today is the day that you start! I will share a few of mine over the next few days. Affirmations are declaring, boldly, positive thoughts of what/who you want to be. For me: "I am Healing and Happiness." -Coco

What do you affirm?

_____
_____
_____
_____
_____
_____
_____
_____
_____
_____
_____
_____
_____
_____
_____

Day Three

"I am Prosperity and Patience." -Coco

I am prosperous in everything that I do. I affirm patience to be able to wait! I know that sometimes we want things to happen overnight, but great things take time.

What do you affirm?

_____
_____
_____
_____
_____
_____
_____
_____
_____
_____
_____
_____
_____
_____
_____
_____
_____
_____

Day Four

"I am Wealth and Success." -Coco

No matter what anyone may say or think, we need money to live on this earth. In order to accomplish the many goals that I have, it takes money. I affirm wealth so that I can accomplish these things. Success looks different for everyone. For me, success is accomplishing the goals that I have set for myself, no matter if I reach one person or one hundred.

What do you affirm?

_____
_____
_____
_____
_____
_____
_____
_____
_____
_____
_____

Day Five

"I am Peace and Positivity." -Coco

For the past few years, I know that you've been hearing, *protect your peace*. I honestly love peace! I don't like drama, people or things that will drain me, therefore; I put out what I expect. If I get anything other than peace, I reject it. That goes for my peace and my positivity.

What do you affirm?

_____
_____
_____
_____
_____
_____
_____
_____
_____
_____
_____
_____

Day 6

"I am Light and Love." -Coco

I have had many difficult trials in my life and there were several times that I could have allowed darkness to overtake me. I could have been bitter, harsh, difficult to deal with, and cruel, but I choose light. I decided that the things that could have ruined me, the things that could have broken me, I allowed to fuel me and hurdle me towards the light. I made the choice to shine, no matter the darkness.

What do you affirm?

_____
_____
_____
_____
_____
_____
_____
_____
_____
_____
_____

Day 7

"I am Confident and Courageous." -Coco

Sometimes we let fear stop us in our tracks for going after the things that we know that we are capable of. Look fear in the eyes and declare that: *Fear Is A Liar!*

Day 8

"I am Fabolous and Fearless." -Coco

There's no one in this world that can stop you, but you! Put on your crown King! Put on your crown Queen! Be fearless and fabulous, as you conqueror your goals!

Day 9

"I am worthy of all good things." -Coco

God has created so many beautiful places and given many of us talents to create some amazing things. He did not intend on just one set of people seeing it! Don't limit yourself. I am worthy of all good things.

Day 10

"I am enough." -Coco

I am not defined by what others think of me or how they view me. I am enough, just as I am!

The next few days will be a little different. Now that you have made some bold affirmations, let's work on some alone time/self-care.

A Few Quotes

"If you are scared, keep going, if you are hungry, keep going, if you want to taste freedom, keep going." - Harriet Tubman (reference day 8)

"No one but me! No matter the highs or lows, no matter which way the wind blows. No matter how hard the glue sticks, no matter how hard the devil kicks, it's me and I will be who I am destined to be." -Shennette Sparks (reference day 17)

"Do not let the behavior of others destroy your inner peace." —Dalai Lama. (reference day 5)

"Courage is the most important of all the virtues because without courage, you can't practice any other virtue consistently." — Maya Angelou (reference day 7)

"Success is walking from failure to failure with no loss of enthusiasm." -- Winston Churchill (reference day 4)

"But my darling, there's no such thing as the light at the end of the tunnel, you must realize that you are the light". – Anonymous (reference day 6)

"Just like there's always time for pain, there's always time for healing." ― Jennifer Brown (reference day 2)

"If you want greater prosperity in your life, start forming a vacuum to receive it." -Catherine Ponder (reference day 3)

Day 11

Today, think of your favorite place and if it's in reach, go there. If not, sit in a quiet place an visualize it. For me, I have a favorite park, though I love all things nature, this particular park is my absolute favorite. What experience did you have?

_____
_____
_____
_____
_____
_____
_____
_____
_____
_____
_____
_____
_____
_____
_____
_____
_____
_____

Day 12

Turn your favorite music on full blast and dance like no one is watching!

Music is uplifting, reduces anxiety, blood pressure, helps with sleep quality, mood, memory, and mental alertness; according to research done by Johns Hopkins. (Hopkins, 2021)

Day 13

This is definitely one that I have to work on myself. It's time to truly, have a seat at a table for one. Get dressed and take yourself out to dinner. Wherever you choose. Don't sit at the bar, sit at a table. Sit with confidence, your body language will command attention (It's not about the attention, it is about having the confidence to dine alone boldly, confidentially and not looking nervous, lonely, or ashamed)! Believe it or not, others view those that have the confidence to dine alone, as powerful people!

_____
_____
_____
_____
_____
_____
_____
_____
_____
_____
_____

Day 14

I remember when I was going to counseling, my counselor, asked me a question, and made me ask myself, every time, I was putting others before I did myself; I'm now going to ask you. Ask yourself, *What Do I Need Today?* Maybe you need to turn your phone off. Maybe you need to not return a call or text. Maybe you just need fifteen minutes of absolute silence. Maybe you need a gut, busting laugh. Whatever you need today, GET IT!

_____
_____
_____
_____
_____
_____
_____
_____
_____
_____
_____
_____
_____

Day 15

Are you living life with gratitude? I know that life happens, and every day is not Strawberry Cheesecake icecream, with Brownies (that's my fav), lmbo, but try to see the good in every situation no matter what! I'm not saying that you aren't going to be sad or cry. What I am saying is that, if you wake up to a flat tire, don't be upset at the flat tire, but thankful that it's just one! Just an example.

Day 16

"Don't waste precious memories on petty moments."-Coco

I remember when I came up with the slogan. I was picking one of my sons up from North Carolina. We were on our way back home on the interstate and there was a car speeding past us. He let his window down to yell at the person in the car for being a jerk and I remember saying those words. When you are out enjoying life or enjoying family and some stranger or even a family member says or does something that tries to disrupt your precious memory don't respond with the petty moment. Don't allow people to get under your skin. Time is precious and we can't get it back. Precious memories are rare, and they are indeed special name a few things that you can do in order to ignore petty moments.

_____
_____
_____
_____

Day 17

"Sometimes you have to do the work that nobody wants to do to prove that you can do the work that everyone does." - Coco

Sounds a bit strange doesn't it? It's not about proving to others that you can do it, it's about proving it to yourself. What's something that you've always wanted to do, that no one else in your circle wants to do? The truth is, it's not that they don't want to do it, they are afraid to do it. They may even try to talk you out of doing it. Jump off the porch and do it (refer back to day 8)!

Day 18

Normalize saying no, with love and without explaining yourself or feeling guilty for doing so. This is something that I had to learn. It's not easy, but it can be done, it needs to be done.

Day 19

"This too shall pass." 2Corinthians 4: 17-18 Irregardless of your belief system, this statement can apply to everyone. Look at your life from five years ago, a year ago, a month ago, look at how far you've come. Take a good look, did situations, pain, or people that weren't meant to be in your life pass? If it has yet to pass, what do you wish, hope, or pray will pass?

_____
_____
_____
_____
_____
_____
_____
_____
_____
_____
_____
_____
_____
_____
_____

Day 20

Well look at you all positive and refreshed! How do you feel? It's time to treat yourself! What haven't you done in a while? You deserve it! I have a saying and I live by this thing: God did not place us on this earth to work and die! Enjoy yourself and don't feel guilty about it!

Day 21

You've made it twenty-one days! How do you feel? Did you learn anything new about yourself? What will you take with you moving forward?

_____
_____
_____
_____
_____
_____
_____
_____
_____
_____
_____
_____
_____
_____
_____
_____
_____
_____
_____
_____
_____
_____
_____
_____

Thank you all so much for spending twenty-one days with me! I hope that this journey and journal has made a positive impact on you. If you would like to share any part of your journal with me, or to leave me a review, feel free to do so in any of the following ways:

Website: www.cocorobertsbooks.com

Facebook: Coco's Corner

Instagram: @CocoRobertsBooks

Twitter: @kissesofcoco

Email: cococamwrites@aol.com

You've completed your 21 days! I wanted to leave you with this: Whatever it is that you desire in life: Write the vision, make it plain! -Habakkuk 2:2

Notes

Notes

www.ingramcontent.com/pod-product-compliance
Lightning Source LLC
Chambersburg PA
CBHW031434040426
42444CB00006B/808